# Hope is Found

To Phyllis:

May your Advent be
filled with hope & joy,
Just like your soul!

—

Phyllis,
May God bring you
the blessings of
hope & family this
hope Advent. Melissa

# Daily Devotions for Advent

## Daniel Hawkins & Melissa Turkett

*To GG.*

*Our beloved matriarch, our rock. Your strength, care and love are the foundation on which the whole Koos/Kenyon/Hawkins/Meyer clan stand. Thank you for loving us so well.*

*-Daniel*

*To my dad.*

*Thanks for embodying and teaching me generosity.*

*-Melissa*

# TABLE OF CONTENTS

# ACKNOWLEDGEMENTS

As we bring to a conclusion the creation of this devotional guide, I am incredibly thankful for family in all its forms that have helped me experience the truth that we are proclaiming in this book.

Thank you to my church family for the ways you help me experience the hope of Advent every year.

Thank you to those friends and colleagues that might as well be family for their encouragement, wisdom and proofing skills. I find hope in my shared life with you.

Thank you to my extended family for the myriad of moments that we have experienced hope over the years (including a number that are captured in these pages).

Thank you to my colleague and friend, Melissa for your dedication to this book, your inspiring words and your passion for Christ. This book is better because we wrote it together.

Finally I'd like to thank "my girls." To my loving and ever-patient wife, April and my two daughters, Abby and Chloe, I want you to know that my life is infinitely better than I deserve because of you. Thank you for your love, your joy and the hope you embody and inspire.

- Daniel

---

This book would not be written without the support of an incredible church. Thank you First United Methodist Church of Cleburne for being a church family that supports me. Thank you for supporting and encouraging creative ventures that allow me to lead in ways that encounter the stranger longing to be neighbor both inside our walls and out.

I would not be the pastor I am today if not for the women in my circle. To the women who have mentored me and shown me what it means to be female clergy I cannot thank you enough. Thank you for showing me when I had no template from my childhood. To the women who are my dear, dear friends, Stacy, Evey, Erin, Joy, and Katie, thank y'all for being the truth tellers in my life.

I am grateful for my friend and peer Rev. Daniel Hawkins. For his leadership of the church where I serve, you are a gift to the staff and the congregation. And of course, for having the spark that would take a sermon series and make it into the book you now hold in your hands.

Lastly, thank you Patrick. Thanks for being my partner-in-adventure and putting up with the times where I insisted on having the lights on while we watch TV so I could work on the cover art. My life is richer because you are in it and you give me the courage to pursue the dreams of my heart. Love you.

- Melissa

# INTRODUCTION

"Oh no!" I think to myself. "I've done it again."

It happens to me every year. Just as the tryptophan from the Thanksgiving turkey wears off and the need for stretchy pants fades away, I look at the calendar and do the math. I realize that I am less than FOUR weeks from Christmas and I am NOT ready! A multitude of feelings wash over me and I find my old holiday friends: stress over getting everything done, the busyness of the "holiday hustle", worry about getting the right present for the right people, and hope that somehow, someway this Advent and Christmas season might be different.

As you open this devotional guide for the first time there is a chance that you have just looked at your calendar and said to yourself "Oh no!" Whether you've experienced that specific internal dialogue or not, I am highly confident that at some point along the way you have found my old friends. If you're looking for a guide to help you find a way to get everything done or get just the right present for the right person, I hate to tell you, but you've bought the wrong book. There are many articles written by infinitely more qualified people that are just a quick google search away.

If you, however, want to say goodbye to your old friends of busyness, stress and worry and make this Christmas different, I believe you've come to the right place. In the pages of this devotional guide we will explore together all of the places where Hope is Found this Advent and Christmas season.

My friend and colleague Rev. Melissa Turkett and I deeply believe that *Hope is Found:*
- *at the dinner table*
- *in the carols we sing*
- *in the stories we tell*
- *around the Christmas Tree*
- *in the candlelight*
- *in the manger*
- *and in the aftermath*

Over the next twenty six days, you'll explore ways we find hope in each of these places this Advent and Christmas Season. Each week you will be given:

- questions to wrestle with
- things to give up
- carols to sing
- prayers to pray
- an invitation to worship.

---

We thank you for being on this journey with us, and we invite you to invest deeply. We believe and trust that when you do, you will find the *hope* God is trying to give you this Advent and Christmas.

Rev. Daniel Hawkins & Rev. Melissa Turkett

Hope is found

# HOPE IS FOUND AT THE DINNER TABLE

## DECEMBER 1

I make the same promise every year at Christmas, and every year I fail…

I tell myself "I will not look more like Santa Claus after Christmas than I did before." You know the look I'm talking about, right??? Lighter wallet… plumper cheeks… rounder belly. In recent years as my beard has gotten more and more grey, the post-Christmas look in the mirror has become even more troubling.

Why is this? Why is it so difficult to leave Advent and Christmas behind the same size you started?

For many questions in this world the answers are multi-faceted, complex and difficult to articulate, but for this question, the answer is profoundly simple. Advent and Christmas are seasons of comfort food and shared tables.

While they may make us look a little more like Santa, the comfort food and shared tables of Advent and Christmas don't just feed our bellies, they feed our souls. Whether we're eating Grandma's pecan pie or we're enjoying the holy guessing game as we fill our plate at the potluck Sunday School Christmas party, the comfort food and shared tables of Advent and Christmas connect us to the people we love and God loves. This week as we get our hearts and souls ready for Christmas we remember that Hope Is Found at the dinner table. Join us as we remember how both Grandma's pecan pie* and the family table connect us to the hope God has for us this Christmas.

*Look ahead to day 5 before you go grocery shopping this week. :)

# DECEMBER 2

## GATHER:

*"When he returned, the servant reported these excuses to his master. The master of the house became angry and said to his servant, 'Go quickly to the city's streets, the busy ones and the side streets, and bring the poor, crippled, blind, and lame.' The servant said, 'Master, your instructions have been followed and there is still room."*

**Luke 14:21-22**

Read: Luke 14:16-24

## GROW:

When I lived in the Susanna Wesley House, an Intentional Christian Community, we had a rule for Community Meal. Our rule was simple. When we invited people we invited them like this, "come any Monday (that's not a holiday) at 6pm." The invitation stood open and our physical doors reflected the same openness. You might think, how on earth did you ever plan? Well, honestly we didn't. We simply prepared food for the people in our home times two. Some weeks we had leftovers, and you better believe they got eaten. Other weeks we had just enough, but never, not once, did we ever run out.

This open invitation did something, it invited the Holy Spirit in to run wild. It led to evenings where neighbor got to know neighbor, pastor got to know pastor, and kids got to find new friends. We hosted old money, new money, and no money. Our dinner table fed every color skin you could imagine. Some evenings the conversations went deep, and other times playing "the floor is lava" with small children was more important. However, one thing remained ever true of our table, it was never empty on a Monday night.

Okay, one time, one time we cancelled the meal because a skunk died under the home and nobody wants to eat dinner in a home that smells like dead skunk. But you know what happened? We loaded up in a couple of cars and we ate snow cones layered with fresh fruit for dinner, our spirits were still fed that night.

Sometimes we miss the gift of gathering around our dinner table. Sometimes we miss the gift of the people at the table. Sometimes we need to be shaken out of the stupor that is found in our normal rhythms to remind us of the gift of hope. In this parable, Christ is reminding us that the gift of hope at our dinner tables is found by throwing open our doors and running out to invite the stranger to come sit at our family dinner tables. This Advent Season we will be reminded time and time again that if we desire to find hope we must be willing to exchange our norms for Christ's norms. It will challenge us. It will lead us to hope, and it will transform us for the sake of Christ.

I have to be honest, now that Patrick and I live on our own again we don't host a weekly community meal, but we still deeply believe in the power of our table. So, we find someone we want to know - a friendship we want to grow or a congregation member whom we are curious about - and we invite them over. Sometimes this means the first date won't work out, so we try again. Sometimes it simply doesn't work out, but we keep identifying people and we keep inviting them to come and eat at our table.

Go:

Take time with these questions today:

In this parable, who is Christ telling you to invite to your table? Will you do it?

# December 3

## Gather:

*"As he was thinking about this, an angel from the Lord appeared to him in a dream and said, "Joseph son of David, don't be afraid to take Mary as your wife, because the child she carries was conceived by the Holy Spirit. {…} When Joseph woke up, he did just as an angel from God commanded and took Mary as his wife."*

**Matthew 1:20, 24**

## Grow:

Some of my favorite memories of childhood are times when we'd gather with our family to celebrate Christmas. One Christmas during elementary school my family gathered along with my aunt, uncle and some of my cousins at Grandma Hawkins's house in St. Joseph, Missouri. One night during our visit, my aunt was in charge of the meal. When the dinner hour came we all gathered around the table; my family, my grandma, my cousins and my uncle. As we gathered my aunt was working to bring the food to the table. That's when it happened… with no warning, my

23

brother Ben screamed!  As my Aunt placed a giant battleship grey hunk of dead cow on the table, Ben followed his scream with a loud question "What is THAT?!?"

Ben was deeply surprised by the roast and the rest of us were deeply surprised by Ben.  While we were mortified at Ben's reaction in the moment (and the truly scary roast that sat before us on the table), that Christmas time dinner is one that lives on in our shared life as a family.  Every time we think of it, it brings a smile to our faces, joy to our hearts and hope for our next meal.

I think this is because God works in unexpected ways when we create the time and space to gather and love as family.

Joseph was surprised by how God was working that first Christmas, but the world was forever changed because he was willing, in the face of a big surprise, to continue to gather and love Mary as family.

## Go:

What unexpected blessing have you received when you gathered and loved as family?

How can you create space to gather and love around the shared table this Advent?

# DECEMBER 4

## GATHER:

*"And fasting is chiefly an aid to prayer, so much so, that it has frequently been found a means, in the hand of God, of confirming and increasing, not one virtue, but also seriousness of spirit, sincerity, sensitivity and tenderness of conscience, deadness to the world, and consequently a love of God, and of every holy and heavenly feeling."*

**John Wesley** [1]

## GROW:

John Wesley was known for fasting on Wednesdays and Fridays during much of his ministry. Today the spiritual discipline of fasting has fallen to the wayside. However, it is still a powerful way to connect with God, and as John Wesley reminds us above, a means for strengthening our prayer life. Fasting is traditionally thought of in terms of food, and who couldn't use a break this Advent from the onslaught of food? But fasting is not limited to food. Fasting can be abstaining from food, technology, speech or gossip, to name just a

---

[1] http://www.biblebb.com/files/jw-001fasting.htm

few. Practicing fasting is to practice denial. When we fast we open space in our life to make more room for God. In that open space, God will show up. God might show you where there is something broken in your life or faith, God might call you to pray for others, or God might simply be with you.

This Advent you will be challenged to dip your toes into the traditional fast of abstaining from food, and over the course of these next weeks you'll be invited to practice fasting in a variety of ways. Our culture has made the Advent season into a season of over-consumption. We get overwhelmed with the never ending shopping lists, the never ending parties to attend, and the never ending preparations to make. In the growing pile of to-do's, we can often miss where hope is tucked away: in the abundance of family, in the gift of time, and in the simple act of presence.

## Go:

Today, fast from 1 meal.

For those for whom this fast is not feasible, or those with small children, consider giving up a snack or dessert today.

# DECEMBER 5

## GATHER:

*"Rejoice in the Lord always; again I will say, Rejoice."*
**Philippians 4:4  NRSV**

## GROW:

As you already know by now, some of my fondest memories from childhood are holidays spent with family. When we would gather we laughed, we played, we told stories and we ate. Because of geography we spent more holidays with my Grandma Koos who lived in our hometown. As the kid who always shopped in the "husky" section of the department store, I LOVED going to Grandma Koos's house. Grandma Koos was an amazing baker, and her pièce de résistance was her pecan pie. The pecans came from her pecan trees and the crust… oh the crust. The crust was light, flaky and buttery.

As you may know, pie crust tends to get tougher the more you handle it. We would swear growing up that

Grandma's crust was so perfect that she must have mixed it and gotten it in the pan without actually touching it.

As I write about these memories, my mouth waters, and my heart is filled with joy. The joy I experience now is equivalent to (or maybe even greater than) the joy experienced in the moments the memories were made.

When Paul says to "rejoice in the Lord always" part of what he is reminding us to do is to look around for the joy that is present in our life daily. How can you remember joy, experience joy and share joy today?

GO:

Today we challenge you to create a moment of joy with those who are close to you. If you need a place to start, gather those you love and make Grandma Koos's pecan pie.

RECIPE:

Crust:

| | |
|---|---|
| 1 1/3 cups of flour, sifted | 1/2 cup shortening |
| 1/2 teaspoon salt | 6 tablespoons ice water |

Mix Flour with salt. Cut in shortening until the mixture looks like small peas. Add water, 1 tablespoon at a time, tossing the flour mixture with a fork. Mixture should leave the sides of the bowl when all of the water has been added and mixed in. Roll crust on floured board. Chill crust in refrigerator for 1 hour.

Filling:

| | |
|---|---|
| 2 cups of pecans, halved | 4 eggs |
| 1 cup light corn syrup | 1 teaspoon vanilla |
| 1/4 teaspoon salt | 3/4 cup sugar |
| 1/2 cup butter | |

Place one 9" pie crust in a pie pan and weight it (dry beans in parchment paper do a great job). Cook at 375° for 8-10 minutes. After cooking remove from oven, remove weights and let cool.

Melt butter and let cool. Beat eggs until well mixed. Add sugar, corn syrup, vanilla and salt. Add melted butter once cool and blend it all together.

Assembly/Baking:

Add pecans to the pie crust. Pour filling over pecans. Cook at 400° for 30 minutes. Reduce heat to

350°. Cook for an additional 35-40 minutes until light brown and the knife comes out clean when inserted into the middle.

Serving:
    Serve with whipped cream and enjoy!

# December 6

## Gather:

> *"God delights when we live in community.*
> *Think symphony, not soloist."*
> **Bob Goff**

## Grow:

Have you ever been "volun-told" to do something? Have you ever heard of a need and noticed that the job had been assigned to you before anyone ever talked to you about it? Maybe you missed a committee meeting and saw in the minutes later that you were the new person in charge of the thing that was critical to your shared work, but no one actually wanted to do.

Being "volun-told" first happened to me in high school. My mom had recently been given a church to pastor and Advent had arrived. That meant she wanted a soloist for every week of Advent to sing a verse of "O Come, O Come Emmanuel" after the lighting of the

Advent Wreath, and guess who got the privilege of doing it every week??? You're right. Me.

For all of Advent I sang the same song over and over again. You'd think we might want to vary it up a bit, but we didn't. It's not like we're short on good Christmas Carols. Give yourself a few seconds, I'm sure you can name five to ten.

1. O Holy Night
2. Away In A Manger
3. The First Noel
4. O come All Ye Faithful
5. Hark The Herald Angels
6. O Little Town Of Bethlehem
7. Hark How the Bells
8. Joy To The World
9. Silver Bells
10. Silent Night

What I later learned was that we sang "O Come, O Come, Emmanuel" over and over again because it is one of our best Advent Carols. It is the song of our hearts as we long and hope for the arrival of the Christ child. In the Church calendar, Advent is a season of **anticipation** and **preparation** for the gift of Christ at Christmas. Christmas (beginning on Christmas Eve) is the season of **celebration** of the Gift of Christ.

The spirit of anticipation and preparation are found in our Advent Carols like "O Come, O Come Emmanuel." They capture our hope and longing for Christ to be reborn; not just once upon a time in a manger far far away, but in our very hearts and lives this Christmas.

## Go:

The songs of our faith speak to our souls. Each week during this journey to Christmas, we've set aside time and space for God to speak to us through song.

So, today, create time to gather with those who are close to you around a piano (or a youtube lyric video) to sing "O Come, O Come Emmanuel" and express the hope that Christ might be reborn in you, your community and all of the world this Christmas.

# December 7

## Gather:

*"After he took his seat at the table with them, he took the bread, blessed and broke it, and gave it to them. Their eyes were opened and they recognized him, but he disappeared from their sight."*

**Luke 24:30-31**

Read: Luke 24:28-32

## Grow:

And then you exclaimed, "I've been looking for you!"

It feels like I say this almost everyday. I bet you do too.

Whether we're searching for our keys, our coworker who seems to always be on the other side of the office, or our favorite Christmas decoration that has yet to be unwrapped, searching is always a part of our lives.

In the season of Advent what are you searching for? Could it be found at your dinner table? In the story from Luke, the disciples, whether they realized it or not, were searching. They were searching for hope, and they found it when Christ broke the bread. This Advent, I invite you to not look for hope walking with your head down through long trudging days, or in the complicated mess of the holiday calendar. Instead, I invite you to find Christ this Advent in the simple act of breaking bread with one another.

## Go:

The seventh day of each week you'll be given a prayer to pray. Our hope is that the prayer will bless you and remind you to find some rest in the midst of your Advent.

## A BLESSING FOR YOUR DINNER TABLE

May God bless this table, its chairs and benches, its familiar scratches and worn wood grain.

May God bless the plates and center pieces that rest upon this table.

May God bless the wholeness of the food upon this table — the farmer who grew it, the rancher that raised it, the hands that prepared it, and the bodies its sustenance will strengthen.

May God bring the stranger to your table, so that the stranger might become neighbor.

May God bring the lost sheep to your table, so that family might be found at your table.

May God bring reconciliation to your table, so that all may find home.

And may God use your table to be a slice of heaven on earth so that God's glory might be, not just seen, but experienced.

Amen.

1/18 · Sunday afternoon, after church, Shara and her new boy friend, Chris, brought lunch and we sat together @ the dining room table, ate, and spent time visiting + getting to know this stranger. He seems to be a fine gentleman, very personable + friendly. He shows much respect + compassion to Shara. It was a great day.

Hope is found at the dinner table

I have always looked forward to hearing the Christmas Cantata @ Church, ever since I was a kid growing up. Mother sang in the choir @ our church and every Christmas she sang "O Holy Night" either solo or duet, so that has always been my favorite. Tears naturally form when I hear or sing it. Today was no different! The choir led by Werler was amazing w/ several strings and wind instruments also.... and Melissa in her beautiful story teller voice, narrating. What a glorious presentation ending with

O Holy Night!

Thank you Lord

# HOPE IS FOUND IN THE CAROLS WE SING

## DECEMBER 8

As I walk down the aisle of the supermarket, it happens. I hear it. I look around and I can tell everyone else can hear it too. As I look at my fellow shoppers faces, it's as if I can hear the internal dialogue in their minds. They say:

"Yes! I've been waiting all year for this."

### or

"PLEASE... can we just wait until after Thanksgiving???"

This same moment happens every year. Just as the last of the halloween candy is pilfered from the shelves for 25% of its original price and the sugar high that has sustained your children for the last week begins to wear off, CHRISTMAS MUSIC arrives.

Have you ever wondered why we are so quick to play Christmas music?

Is it because there is no good Thanksgiving music? (*think about it... when was the last time you sang a Thanksgiving Classic???*)

Is it simply because our retailers want to extend our shopping season as long as possible?

Both of these are true to a certain extent, but they don't really explain why we play our Christmas songs so early in the year. We can't help but hit play on all of our Christmas playlists because *Hope Is Found* in the carols we sing this time of the year. The joyful beat of our children's favorites has our hearts dashing through the snow. The jubilant exclamations of our favorite carols fill our souls; leaving us crying "O Come, O

Come, Emmanuel" and longing to "Go Tell It on the Mountain" all at the same time.

Join us this week as we explore the carols we sing, and how they help us find the hope we long for this Christmas.

# DECEMBER 9

## GATHER:

*"Sing to God; sing praises to the Lord;*
*dwell on all his wondrous works!"*

**Psalm 105:2**

## GROW:

We've all heard the icebreaker question, "What would be your superpower?" When I lead icebreakers I like to flip that question on its head, "What would your super villain power be?" and I'm always ready with mine. I would want to have Ursula's (yes from the Little Mermaid) ability to steal voices and make them her own. I would collect Ellie Holcomb, Lisa Gungor, and Lauren Daigle's voices to start. I'd be unstoppable on the radio charts with their powerhouse voices. But the reality is I'm more of a story teller than a singer, mostly because my voice range is closer to a tenor's than an alto's and I'm tone-impaired. Now let me be clear, I still love to sing and sing out with my whole being, just as long as no microphone is involved.

Well, whether you are completely tone-deaf or a starring soloist in the season's Christmas Cantata, we all have experienced the unique way music can make us feel, whether we are singing it or receiving it. Advent has a way of drawing the story tellers and the singers together - the story tellers to bring their words and the singers to bring their melodies. The result is some of the most memorable music that the whole world sings as the air grows chilled and the spirit of the season sets in. We sing songs with clear narratives of that first Christmas Eve in "Silent Night," we go on the journey with the Wise Men in "We Three Kings," and we join the celebration when we sing "Angels We Have Heard on High." Advent is a time where our stories and our songs weave together seamlessly.

So this Advent, I'll keep standing in the chancel between two talented singers harmonizing on the Doxology while I try to just stay on pitch in the traditional service. I'll keep walking the halls during the weekdays enjoying the melodies flowing out of the sanctuary as our Contemporary Worship Leader practices guitar or piano. And I'll keep going home to my husband's booming voice projecting out into the evening breeze carrying tidings of good joy. I'll also keep telling my stories in sermons, <u>office drop-bys,</u> and with the stranger in line at the grocery store (I'm a pastor, no one here is surprised by that last one). And this season, I'll sing and appreciate the way our work as story tellers and singers come together to tell the story of a baby born one night in Bethlehem.

## Go:

The world needs the birth of that baby, the birth of Jesus. What carol will you sing for the whole world, so that the world might hear its good news?

# DECEMBER 10

## GATHER:

*"The Word became flesh and blood, and moved into the neighborhood. We saw the glory with our own eyes, the one-of-a-kind glory, like Father, like Son, Generous inside and out, true from start to finish."*

**John 1:14 *The Message***

## GROW:

One of the most powerful moments of every Advent season comes at the end of the Christmas Eve Service. The lights dim. We light our candles. The light of Christ is lifted high, and all as one we sing "Silent Night, Holy Night. All is calm. All is bright."

In this moment Advent meets Christmas. Christ has moved into the neighborhood. Our hope in and longing for the coming of Christ turn into celebration that on this night Christ is being reborn in our hearts, lives and world. It is beautiful. It is holy. It is moving, and it is profoundly peaceful. In this moment, Emmanuel has come. God is with us.

45

In 2014, Adam Hamilton, a noted United Methodist pastor and author, wrote a book called Not a Silent Night. Part of what Hamilton invites us to do in this book is reimagine our idealized image of that very first Christmas Eve.

With this invitation, Hamilton got me thinking about and reflecting on the birth of my oldest daughter, Abby. Her birth was a moment in my life that I'll never forget. She made me a father. It was beautiful, moving and holy… but even in a great hospital with the best medical care available, it was not as peaceful, idyllic or calm as we often depict the birth of Jesus.

Jesus was born in a first century barn. There were no attending physicians, no nurses and no pain meds. There wasn't even good air conditioning to keep Mary comfortable. They were surrounded by beasts of burden, and after he was born he was wrapped in a blanket and placed in a feed trough. The night was sweaty, painful, loud and likely a little scary.

I don't want this to discourage you. I don't want it to be a holy buzzkill. Rather, I hope what you read is a profound word of hope. Hope is found in the beauty of Silent Night, but also in the truth that lies just below the surface. In the messiness of the first Christmas, there is great good news! Just as Emmanuel has come in our holy, beautiful and powerful experiences of worship, Emmanuel has come in our messiness. The good news of Christmas is that Christ is not just reborn into our moments of perfection, but also into our moments of deep imperfection.

## Go:

Where in your life is Christ trying to "move into the neighborhood" and offer rebirth?

# DECEMBER 11

## GATHER:

*"Happy are those who find wisdom and those who gain understanding. Her profit is better than silver, and her gain better than gold."*

**Proverbs 3:13-14**

## GROW:

If you are wise enough to have obtained a copy of this book, you are likely wise enough to know some of the most important fundamental truths of life; like how to properly squeeze a tube of toothpaste or how to correctly place a role of toilet paper. You are wise enough to know that civilized humanity doesn't just squeeze a tube of toothpaste from the middle or hang the toilet paper "back behind" (it is properly hung in a way that leaves the paper hanging over the top. It's in the patent![2])

---

[2] https://www.businessinsider.com/patent-shows-right-way-to-hang-toilet-paper-2015-3

For many centuries, long before there was modern toothpaste or toilet paper, there was another fundamental truth of life that all wise people just understood... when to begin singing Christmas Carols. Our 21st century debate centers around whether they should be sung before or after Thanksgiving. For many of our mothers and fathers in the faith, this debate would be seen as just plain silly. It would be like debating where in the middle of the toothpaste tube is an acceptable place to squeeze from. Both sides of the argument are just plain wrong.

This is because, for centuries it was the official practice and theology of the Church that Christmas Carols should not be sung until Christmastide, the season in the church calendar that actually begins on Christmas.

To our modern sensibilities, this seems silly. Why would we begin singing Christmas Carols AFTER Christmas??? Truthfully, our mothers and fathers in the faith weren't trying to be party poopers. They just knew our human impulse to jump too quickly to celebration, and that when we did, we missed out on the power of Advent. We missed out on the power of waiting, anticipation and hoping for the coming of Christ.

## Go:

So, today we invite you to fast from Christmas Carols. Embrace the powerful Advent Carols like "O Come, O Come Emmanuel," and "Come Thou Long Expected Jesus." In doing so, you will create space in your soul to embrace the hope and anticipation that God is bringing this Advent. Doing so will help you experience Christmas in an even more profound way this year.[3]

---

[3] If you need some Advent Carol inspiration check out this playlist:
https://open.spotify.com/playlist/6eySVfzgF7Tjb2d0ugXFBf

# DECEMBER 12

## GATHER:

*"Sing lustily and with a good courage. Beware of singing as if you were half dead, or half asleep; but lift up your voice with strength. Be no more afraid of your voice now, nor more ashamed of its being heard, than when you sung the songs of Satan."*

**John Wesley**

## GROW:

I just love John Wesley (which I guess is a good thing for a United Methodist Church Pastor!!!). Over the course of his ministry he gave humanity many gifts:

- life giving theology,
- an understanding of God's grace that speaks to every stage of our life of faith,
- some real pearls of wisdom regarding our physical health in his book entitled "Primitive Physick" (Seriously...google it. There are some really great gems like: "hold a live puppy constantly on the belly" for an obstructed bowel.).

BUT one of my favorite gifts from John Wesley are his instructions for singing that are helpfully printed in the front of every United Methodist Hymnal[4]. My favorite rule is printed in the Gather section above. While I think that it is useful instruction for everyday, it is especially relevant for the times when we go Christmas Caroling.

Most years, in the churches I serve, we gather as a church family in mid-December to fill up our bellies at a Nacho Bar and go Christmas caroling at a local nursing home. Why do we have nachos to eat? Yes, in part it is because we are in Texas, but mostly, it is because our caroling is "Nacho Average Caroling."

Why are you groaning???

That's a great pun!

Anyway... I think that part of the reason that I love our caroling is that when we go caroling at our local nursing home everyone, residents and church members alike, is singing as John Wesley instructs. We're singing

---

[4] Wesley's instructions for singing can also be found at https://www.umcdiscipleship.org/resources/wesleys-directions-for-singing

with great gusto.  No one would accuse us of being half dead or half asleep, and this is important because we have good news to proclaim!  Emmanuel, Christ is with us!

## Go:

So, today go caroling.  Grab your kids. Grab some friends.  Grab somebody and go singing.  And remember, as good ole' JW says "Sing lustily and with a good courage. Beware of singing as if you were half dead, or half asleep; but lift up your voice with strength. Be no more afraid of your voice now, nor more ashamed of its being heard, than when you sung the songs of Satan."

# December 13

## Gather:

*"Glory to God in the highest, and on earth peace, good will toward men."*

**Luke 2:14 (KJV)**

## Grow:

Thank the Lord for George Whitefield and the invention of moveable type by Gutenberg! Without them we would not have come to love Charles Wesley's "Hark! The Herald Angels Sing" the way we do today. It is a staple for the Christmas holidays.

Do you know what a Welkin is? Me neither, but I looked it up for us. A Welkin is the "sky or firmament," and in Charles' meaning it is where the angels reside. In the original version of "Hark! The Herald Angels Sing" the first couplet was:

*Hark how all the Welkin rings*
*Glory to the King of Kings,*

It just doesn't have the same ring to it, does it?

Thankfully the Wesley brothers' friend George Whitefield got his hands on it and changed the opening line to the familiar words that we know and love today:

> *Hark! The herald angels sing*
> *Glory to the newborn King.*

Charles also originally set the lyrics to a slow and solemn tune and that remained its tune until the 1840s when Felix Mendelssohn composed a cantata celebrating the 400th anniversary of the invention of moveable type by Johannes Gutenberg. Mendelssohn combined some stanzas and added the repeating first line to fit his more uplifting tune he composed for the song. As a result the tune grew in popularity and notoriety.[5]

So even if he needed a little help, Charles Wesley gave us a gift in this beloved carol. A carol that brings us right into the middle of the story, a story that has cosmic implications, a story that matters in the heavens

---

[5] https://www.umcdiscipleship.org/resources/history-of-hymns-hark-the-herald-angels-sing

and the Earth, a story that reminds us of the grand importance of the Incarnation (that the Divine would come down to Earth). In this carol the birth has already happened and we are ushered into the celebration of what Charles originally titled, "Hymn for Christmas Day." Can't you feel the celebration when you sing it? I find myself rocking forward onto the balls of my feet and wanting to push up to my tip toes. The joy of the song builds in me, and I want to dance for joy and celebration with the Angels. I want to shout the quoted Scripture "God and sinner reconciled." Charles' own translation and theological summary of Luke 2:14.

## Go:

Today, whether in the car on the way to work, at home with the family, or with a group of carolers, sing out in celebration "Hark! The Herald Angels Sing."

# December 14

## Gather:

*"And Mary said, 'My soul magnifies the Lord,'"*
**Luke 1:46 (NRSV)**

Read: Luke 1:46-55

## Grow:

Disclaimer: I'm about to step on some toes, so watch out. I make no apologies.

Mary Did you Know?

**YES!**

Read your Bible. Mary knew!

I'll step down from my soapbox now, but if you can't tell "Mary Did You Know" does not make my top 40 favorite Christmas songs. That said, one of my favorite Christmas songs that often goes overlooked in the Advent season is Mary's song. Yes, Mary wrote a song.

We find it in Luke's Gospel and we often call it "Mary's Magnificat." I love her carol because it teaches us so much about the mother of Jesus.

Did you read the whole passage? Doesn't it sound like a Psalm? She clearly spent time in the temple. When you hear Jesus speak do you not hear her influence? Like in Luke 4:18-19 or anytime Jesus tells people the most important commandment? Love the Lord your God with everything you have, that's Deuteronomy 6, and it is a prayer mothers would pray over their children when they laid them down to sleep.

Mary was a good mother, and a faithful Jew. Mary understood what was happening to her, and she trusted God so much she sang about it. Mary could have been killed for being pregnant out of wedlock, especially while she was engaged to another man. Let's be honest, when we're in deep trouble do we trust God so much we want to compose a hymn? Mary's carol inspires me to trust God in every season of my life.

GO:

Receive this prayer as inspired by "Mary's Magnificat" and may you find some rest from your holiday lists today.

58

Holy Christ,
Born of a woman,
may we give thanks to you,
for the women in our lives,
who have taught us to exalt your holy name.

Incarnate God,
raised by a mother,
May we trust you beyond our wildest imagination,
this advent season,
may we remember you exalt the lowly,
and send the proud and rich away empty-handed.

Beloved Jesus,
resting in his mother's embrace,
remind us that you will embrace us
and shower mercy upon us
just as you have done for our ancestors,
to Abraham and to Abraham's descendants forever.
Amen.

Hope is found in the carols we sing

# HOPE IS FOUND IN THE STORIES WE TELL

## DECEMBER 15

If you have children there is likely a movie that you can quote by heart, not because you do or don't enjoy it, but because your child watched it on repeat time and time again. The story my small soul needed to watch, hear, and sing with time and time again was Disney's *The Little Mermaid*. I think my parents cringed when they'd hear the credits begin to roll, followed by little steps pattering towards the TV where an unmistakable click would resound followed by the whir of the VHS tape beginning to rewind then stop. Followed by that opening sound still played out on any Disney movie, the building of an orchestra as Tinkerbell flits over

Cinderella's castle trailing fairy dust to be captured in an arch across the sky. All of this would go on all day if not for parental intervention. Even through my college days there were certain movies that could always be popped on to play in the background - *Pitch Perfect* for a guaranteed laugh or *Jane* for a good cry. But more recently in life, re-watching movies seems like a fading tradition. It only takes the click of a couple buttons and libraries of more movies than could be consumed in a lifetime are available (and if they're not on one of my subscriptions then iTunes has it for rent).

We are a people that consume more stories, but we are also not revisiting the important stories as often. Advent is a season where we as the Global Christian Community gather around one of our most important stories, the story of God come down to earth in the form of a babe. In Matthew's Gospel we are reminded of how many important stories, stories worth retelling and rehearing our whole lifetime, happened to lead up to this beautiful moment that we are preparing our hearts to celebrate on the 25th. Though Matthew's list of names, the genealogy of Jesus found in chapter 1, seem like an endless dry list, each name has a story to tell, and many of those stories are captured in our scriptures.

This week we'll be reminded of the power of story, the gift of old favorites and new stories, and the hope that is found in the stories we tell. So tonight I think I'll curl up and revisit an old favorite, *The Little Mermaid*, and once the credits roll, instead of hitting rewind, I'll revisit one other story worth hearing, the story of Jesus' genealogy as found in Matthew 1.

## DECEMBER 16

GATHER:

*"Look! A virgin will become pregnant and give birth to a
son, and they will call him, Emmanuel.
(Emmanuel means "God **with** us.)"*

**Matthew 1:23**

GROW:

Do you have a person in your life who is impossible
to shop for?

You know the person. That special someone in your
life that - no matter how hard you try to get them
something creative, new or original that they will love -
you know your gift giving efforts will always fail.

My dad is THAT guy in my life. As a highly
successful professional, he is impossible to buy gifts for.
When it comes to *stuff,* if he wants it either:

1. He already has it

    or

2. I *can't* afford it

This is life with my dad.

Several years ago when I was wrestling with what to give my dad for Christmas, I heard a pastor tell a story of a young man who knew my pain. His dad was just like mine, impossible to buy for, and yet somehow he'd managed to buy his dad the *perfect* gift.

As I heard the story, I was struck dumb.

He was brilliant. The gift he got for his dad was creative, new, original and deeply meaningful. This young man got his coffee loving dad a pound of coffee... and a simple note. In the note the young man informed his father that this coffee was special. The dad could only drink it with his son. The young man closed his note by telling his dad that he deeply admired him, and wanted to hear the stories of his life that made him the man he was.

He captured the beauty and essence of the gift of Christmas: presence. The gift of Christmas is that Emmanuel has come! God is present with us.

Every year we struggle to find the right gift for the right person. What if the right gift were as simple as sitting down with someone we love to hear their stories and share our own?

## Go:

Today ask yourself:

Who do I need to reconnect with today?

Who in my life do I need to share stories with?

# December 17

## Gather:

*"Hear, O Israel: The Lord is our God, the Lord alone. You shall love the Lord your God with all your heart, and with all your soul, and with all your might. Keep these words that I am commanding you today in your heart. Recite them to your children and talk about them when you are at home and when you are away, when you lie down and when you rise. Bind them as a sign on your hand, fix them as an emblem on your forehead, and write them on the doorposts of your house and on your gates."*

**Deuteronomy 6:4-9 (NRSV)**

## Grow:

The Shema, it's the passage you just read from Deuteronomy 6:4-9, and it literally means "to hear" in Hebrew. That hearing, to shema, became an important reminder for the Israelite people to keep God first and it was so important to them that these verses in Deuteronomy became a prayer that was prayed in the morning and the evening.

The Shema truly captures the heart of the Israelite people in such a succinct and poignant way. The Shema, this prayer, can be found written across the narrative of the Old Testament. This prayer helped the Israelite people create laws and poetry, covenant and songs, all for the purpose of building a distinct culture, a set apart culture. At the root of every law or song was the seed of the Shema, a prayer that would be bound to their arms and nailed to their doorposts.

The narrative of the Old Testament continues to the New Testament, it is woven in the fabric of Jesus' life (reread Deuteronomy 6:5 and I bet you hear Jesus' voice) and his birth. Think about it, each Gospel begins with telling a story. Matthew's Gospel starts with a long list of genealogy leading up to Jesus, and each of those names represents an entire story that leads us to the birth of the Messiah. John's Gospel begins with the philosopher's poetic summary of all the stories from the Old Testament now woven together leading to this obvious outcome of the birth of light, the birth of a Savior.

The Hebrew people, God's chosen people, are a people of story because in each person's story is a chance to allow God's story to be told. So telling stories is an essential part of worship. Storytelling begins the Shabbat (or sabbath). We as Christ followers are a continuation of the Hebrew people, every time we tell a story — the story of our day, the story of our family, even a Bible story — we have an opportunity to share the story of Christ.

## Go:

This Christmas season, may our stories each reflect the Shema, God's invitation to hear God's story.

So, the simple question then to be asked is, what is your story? Consider writing it down so that generations may come to hear the good news of Christ in the narrative of your life.

# DECEMBER 18

## GATHER:

*Clarence the angel: "Strange, isn't it? Each man's life touches so many other lives. When he isn't around he leaves an awful hole, doesn't he?"*

**It's a Wonderful Life**

## GROW:

Every Christmas season growing up my family had a list of must watch Christmas movies. My dad insisted on *A Christmas Story*, I insisted on *The Grinch* (the original animated version), and my mom insisted on *It's a Wonderful Life*. It didn't feel like the Christmas season was complete until we had watched at least these three movies together as a family.

I can see the crinkle in the corner of my father's eye and hear his chuckle as the father from *A Christmas Story* receives his major prize. I can remember my family singing along to "You're a Mean One Mr. Grinch" as the Grinch cut red fabric to become his Santa suit.

And even though it was my mom's pick, *It's a Wonderful Life*, has become one of my must watch movies for the holiday season. Do you remember that scene at the end of the film where George Bailey is back in his family home gathered with all his family? I would always look over at my mom who would be dabbing the corner of her eyes with a bandana my father handed her. I can remember feeling my heart grow warm and tingly. Pretty soon that feeling spread to my small mouth stretching it into a wide toothy smile, while my eyes filled to the brim with water that my eyelashes tried to blink back before it burst over becoming tears.

There's power in the story a movie can tell, but there's a greater power when we allow our life to tell a story. So though yes, movies are a part of the fabric of my Christmas holidays, it would be a shame if I missed out on the beauty of the season, the real life moments that could stretch my smile and fill my eyes in my own life. The movies wouldn't be as special if it weren't for my father's laughter, my mother's alto voice and tears, or even my childlike joy.

## Go:

So to bring balance to your holidays, fast from your normal evening rhythms and look for the emotions your favorite Christmas movie brings you (hope, wonder, tears, laughter, joy) in your day today.

# DECEMBER 19

## GATHER:

*"We do not draw people to Christ by loudly discrediting what they believe, by telling them how wrong they are and how right we are, but by showing them a light that is so lovely that they want with all of their hearts to know the source of it."*

**Madeline L'Engle**

## GROW:

The interruption was so forceful that I was left without words. It was jarring. As I turned to the source of the interruption, I noticed that everyone around me was doing the same thing. As our attention focused, the loud and fuzzy disruption crystalized into sharp and biting words of judgement.

That night, as I stood on the street corner, I was greeted with words of judgment, critique and righteous anger that spewed forth with such fervor that it was clear that the street corner preacher was absolutely certain that I and everyone within earshot was the embodiment of the worst kind of sin and brokenness found in humanity.

As a pastor, all I wanted to do was tell him to STOP.

I'm deeply convinced that Madeline L'Engle is absolutely right that we cannot and will not draw people to Christ by shouting them down, "loudly discrediting what they believe, by telling them how wrong they are and how right we are." We need to show and tell a story that is so beautiful that others can't help but be drawn to its source.

While I have rarely experienced the same vitriol and judgement I experienced on that street corner during the Advent and Christmas seasons (thanks be to God!!!), I have experienced - more often than I'd like to admit - well meaning Christians using their voice and their platform to grouchily advocate that we should "put the Christ back in Christmas" and avoid saying "Happy Holidays."

I can't help but wonder how much more effective would our witness be if instead of grouchily arguing that we need to "put the Christ back in Christmas" we would simply show the love of Christ, God among us, who came to love and redeem the entirety of humanity.

What if we told the story of God's love with our actions and met people in their need this Christmas?

## Go:

This week we are celebrating that hope is found in the stories we tell. How can you tell the Christmas story with your actions and service this week?

# DECEMBER 20

## GATHER:

*"...the conquering King, and the crucified Lord...has come to bring peace and justice to the dispossessed of the land. That is why the slave wanted to 'go tell it on de mountain.'"*

**Dr. James H. Cone**

## GROW:

When I think of "Go Tell It on the Mountain," I think of dulcimers and banjos, mandolins and folksy singers. My favorite rendition of the song is sung by a folksy-Americana, sitting around the living room, style band. The song can be found on *A Neighborly Christmas* being sung by Drew Holcomb & the Neighbors.

Though I think of this Christmas carol as folksy in nature, it was actually originally written as a negro spiritual. "Go Tell It on the Mountain" can first be found in print in *Religious Folk Songs of the Negro, as Sung on The Plantations* listed as a "Christmas Plantation Song". And this American Christmas carol may have been lost to the memory of time, had it not been for The

Fisk Jubilee Singers. These singers are credited with saving the Negro spiritual and saving their university that was on the edge of closing by touring and raising money for the university[6]. This truly is an incredible story that I am not doing justice, but I encourage you to read more on it by reading the article found in the footnote.

A song born of slavery reminds us of the power of the story we remember every Advent, every season we wait for our Savior to come, for a child to be born. We must remember that the Israelites themselves spent years in slavery and when they spoke of the coming Messiah they were placing their hope in the one who would free them from their physical chains. The Israelite and the American slave both understood deeply the power of hope, and the desire to share that hope from the mountain tops.

This Advent, let us celebrate the deeply American carol that reminds each person of the excitement we build as we move towards Christmas Day. A carol that's meaning brings hope to the slave and joy to the child.

---

[6] https://www.umcdiscipleship.org/resources/history-of-hymns-go-tell-it-on-the-mountain

## Go:

Sing along in your car or living room, "Go Tell It on the Mountain," and give thanks for the Messiah that breaks chains and sets us free.

# December 21

GATHER:

*"In God we live, move, and exist."*
**Acts 17:28a**

GROW:

"Dancing CATS… on a COAT RACK???"

"Dancing cats on a coat rack?"

"Dancing cats on a coat rack."

This is all that I can think as I sit in the middle of my parents living room with all of the eyes of my extended family on me. From across the room I catch glances from my mother and my grandmother. They have great hope and expectation in their eyes. My cousins and my uncle are looking at me with deep pity in their eyes. My dad and brother are still shocked and their faces haven't moved in what feels like forever.

79

I don't know what to do. Do I cry? Do I laugh? Is this a prank? Am I at the center of an elaborate joke, or are they really being serious?

I'm a 19 year old college student and I have just opened my Christmas present from my grandmother. Gifts from grandma are often the highlight of Koos family Christmas, and the gifts are often memorable.

This is certainly memorable. What sits before me is a dancing cat coat rack ready to be mounted to the wall of my first college apartment. There are cats of all kinds; brown cats, black and white cats, and orange cats. And they are all doing the can-can with their arms wrapped around their shoulders, one leg lifted high to hold the coats. It is a sight to see.

I don't want to be judgmental of the "cat" people for whom this was manufactured - in fact it would have been a lovely gift for your favorite 85 year old "cat lady" - but for a 19 year old who hated cats and was still trying to find his way in the world, it was an epic FAIL (sorry Grandma!).

While this story was painful in the moment and caused me to wonder how well my family knew me, in recent years this story has taken its place in the canon of stories we tell when we get together as a family at Christmas. Today we laugh. We smile, and in the telling of the story we are reminded of the power of Christmas to unite us as a family even when we think that everything has gone wrong.

When we allow ourselves to tell our stories, even the difficult ones, we are blessed to discover that hope is found in the stories we tell.

## Go:

As you pray today, we invite you to pray:

Loving God, the co-author of the stories of our lives, we thank you for the gift of our stories. Help us to notice how you are alive and at work in our stories. Inspire us through our stories, and empower us to share our stories with the people we encounter in our lives. Amen.

Hope is found in the stories we tell

# Hope is found around the Christmas Tree

## December 22

There's something about the warm glow of lights on a Christmas tree that invites a flood of memories: children ripping open wrapping paper, the weary eyes of parents on Christmas morning, or the smile of a grandmother holding the newest grandchild. Hope is found around the Christmas tree in the twinkle of ornaments gleaming in the light, the star sitting proudly on top of the tree, and smells perfuming the air.

This week we draw to the close of Advent and we'll find hope as we gather around our Christmas trees. As we approach the birth of Christ it can be tempting to skip these final readings or jump to the end, but stick with it. Linger in this Advent season a few days more as you encounter the hope that we find in the traditions found in our Christmas trees, the people gathered at our Christmas trees, and the Savior that meets us at our Christmas trees. This final week will even take us one day past Advent to see that hope does not abandon us as we take our Christmas trees down.

Today find time to sit at your Christmas tree and read the Christmas Story (Luke 2:1-21).

# DECEMBER 23

## GATHER:

*"What came into being through the Word was life, and the life was the light for all people. The light shines in the darkness, and the darkness doesn't extinguish the light."*

**John 1:3b-5**

## GROW:

Gathering around the Christmas tree is one of those quintessential Christmas activities. Christmas doesn't seem to be complete without gathering together with the people you love around the Christmas tree. We cannot imagine Christmas without it, but did you know that for hundreds of years Christians celebrated the birth of Christ without trees, ornaments or lights?

For many years Christianity was geographically grounded around the Mediterranean Sea, and during this period there were no Christmas trees. In fact, through much of early Christianity the primary celebration of the Christian year was Easter. The celebration of Christmas paled in comparison to the celebration of Easter.

The celebration of Christmas grew as Christianity expanded in the years that followed. Evergreen trees were first linked to the celebration of Christmas as Christianity expanded to Northern Europe. Christian missionaries discovered that the Celts and other Nordic religions celebrated the coming of the winter solstice because it meant that days would begin to get longer. Each day a little more light would return, ushering in the new life of spring and beating back the darkness of winter. These Nordic religions marked the winter solstice by decorating the largest evergreen that marked the center of the village.[7]

Does the "expanding light that beats back darkness and gives life to the world" idea sound familiar? (hint: see the words of John above). It sounded familiar to the Christian missionaries seeking to expand Christianity into Northern Europe. These missionaries worked to connect the local thanksgiving for the expanding light of the winter solstice to the universal work of God in

---

[7] For a deeper dive into the history of trees and Christmas go to: https://robbell.podbean.com/e/alexander-shaia-on-the-mythic-power-of-christmas/

Christ. Pretty soon, the large evergreens trees that were used to mark the annual arrival of the winter solstice were being used to mark and celebrate the eternal and life-giving light of Christ.

## Go:

As you gather around your Christmas tree tonight, how is the light of Christ making new life in your life today?

Hope is found around the Christmas tree

# Hope is found in the candlelight

## December 24

### Christmas Eve

*"The angel said, "Don't be afraid! Look! I bring good news to you—wonderful, joyous news for all people. Your savior is born today in David's city. He is Christ the Lord."*

**Luke 2:10-11**

Grow:

It happens every year. I just can't help it.

My throat catches. My eyes fill. I don't think I can speak, and yet somehow I can sing like there is no tomorrow.

As the lights dim, the giant Christmas tree twinkles in the background, the sounds of "Silent Night" echo off the walls of the church, and the taste of Holy Communion still lingers in my mouth, I light my candle, share it with my neighbor and I raise my candle high. The light of Christ shines forth in the darkness. In this moment, I can hardly speak, but I can't help but sing. In this moment, my eyes fill and yet I see the truth clearly. In this moment, the hope of Christmas is real. The light has come, and it will outshine any darkness.

This moment... it is beautiful. It is holy. It is overwhelming.

This moment is the embodiment of the life I am called to live:

> filled with Christ,
> living in community,
> my soul singing,
> receiving the light of Christ,
> sharing the light with my neighbor,
> then pressing forth into the darkness allowing the light of Christ to lead the way.

Every Christmas Eve, I hope and pray that more and more people get to experience this moment because when we experience this moment all of the other moments of our lives are different.

## GO:

Today's question is simple. How are you making sure you have this moment? Who are you bringing with you?

Hope is found in the candlelight

# HOPE IS FOUND IN THE MANGER

## DECEMBER 25

### CHRISTMAS DAY

GATHER:

> *"But Mary treasured up all these things and
> pondered them in her heart."*
>
> **Luke 2:19**

GROW:

*A Christmas Parable*

Once upon a time, there was a crib and all in the land
knew that the crib was meant for a king. But one day a

carpenter passed by and declared that this small quaint crib did not do justice for the king it was meant to serve. So the carpenter declared to the kingdom, "I will build the finest crib of finest wood for our future king." The kingdom applauded the care of the carpenter. So the carpenter set out and built the finest crib of wood any had ever seen. But when the painter spied the plain wooden crib, the painter declared to the kingdom that this crib would not do to capture the imagination of the small king. So the painter took the crib and painted his finest masterpiece on the crib and the kingdom declared, "surely now this is the fittest crib for any king." But the kingdom's jeweler scoffed and declared to the kingdom that, "No king should be so poorly dressed even in infancy." So the jeweler set out to adorn the crib with the kingdom's finest jewels. And once the jeweler set the crib in front of the kingdom, the kingdom declared, "surely now this crib is ready for a king." And so the people waited for the arrival of a king. Years passed and no king was born, the jewels began to dull, the paint began to chip, and the wood even began to creak when the crib rocked.

But where was the king?

The shepherds of the kingdom knew. You see the crib that was meant for the king had been placed in the barn for the animals. Cows, donkeys and even sheep had eaten from this crib. And on one special night a woman laid her newborn child in the crib, and the shepherds met the king the kingdom had been long awaiting.

The day is here! Advent has ended and we no longer await the coming, for the king has come, our Savior is born! Hope has been found at our dinner tables, in the carols we sang together, in the stories we told, and gathered around our Christmas trees. Today hope is found at the manger. Hope needs no money, no ambition, no fancy wrappings or trappings for its promises to be found. Our great treasure lays not in a golden, gilded cradle, but in a simple manger made of wood and filled with dried hay. Our hope is found in the birth of Emmanuel, Christ the king come to earth.

Remember today that Christ is the treasure we have been hopefully and expectantly awaiting.

## Go:

Today the challenge is simple, remember the treasure is in the people not the things. Be present with the people around you, in the simple moments you share with one another, and in the promise that hope is found in Christ.

# HOPE IS FOUND IN THE AFTERMATH

## EPILOGUE

And now here you are staring at the aftermath. It looks like the Grinch himself has visited your home. There's evidence of where a tree with tinsel stood. There's that broken ornament you sat on the counter and haven't moved yet. There's still some torn wrapping paper about, and yes is that, it is, more tinsel. The only difference between your home and the Grinch's is the stack of storage boxes staring back at you; as you find excuse after excuse to not move those boxes back to their 11 month a year residence in the attic or garage (okay truly 10 months by the time you put them away).

The reality is that when Christmas is over - the family and friends have returned home, the decorations have returned to their place in the attic, and the bill rolls in - we can feel empty.

Hear the good news, CHRIST IS BORN! The celebration of his birth may be put away, but the hope that Christ's birth brought into the world all those years ago still holds true for us this day. Hold true to this promise in this new season of Christmas Tide. The celebration that is now packed away still holds hope for your life today. Christ the Incarnate's birth is here to stay with us. The Kingdom of God is sewn across the earth through the full work of Christ and faithful disciples who usher in the Kingdom one faithful act at a time. In the aftermath, may you find hope in being a deeply committed disciple of Jesus Christ. May you walk faithfully with the Incarnate Christ the next 12 months as you meet him again and again at dinner table, in singing, in stories, and even in mangers and Christmas trees.

Now go one final time, and receive this benediction for your Christmas-tide:

As you stand in the midst of the chaos of the aftermath:
of dishes to be washed,
decorations to come down,

and rooms to be set to right,
Pause for a moment
and let these words reverberate in your soul,
Christ has come,
hope is found.
Christ has come,
hope is found.
Christ has come,
hope is found.
Amen.

---

Thank you so much for spending your Advent with us; it has been our joy to write this devotional. We have been praying for you, even all the way back in July when we first sat down to put ideas on a dry erase board in hopes that a book might come forth from those initial thoughts and ideas. From the initial blistering hot days of July and August, to the editing days of fall and it's reprieve from the Texas heat, we have prayed that the work we do is faithful to God and to you, our reader.

We hope this Advent season filled you with the anticipation, excitement, wonder, and (of course) hope that comes when we stay connected to the story of Christ. We hope that you made new memories this Advent season from baking pies, to singing carols, who's story you now know, and even to a rare quiet moment of reflection. We hope that each of these memories pointed you towards the greatest hope found on Christmas morning, the birth of Christ.

And lastly we hope you walk away from this book knowing this: the truth of Advent, the promise-fulfilled on Christmas morning, is not just for one season a year. Even though we do a really good job of remembering and celebrating it once a year, hope is found in Christ everyday.

Rev. Daniel Hawkins & Rev. Melissa Turkett

ADDITIONAL RESOURCES:

To hear an audio version of this devotional guide listen to the Gather Grow Go Podcast. You can find it in Apple Podcasts, on Soundcloud or at www.fumccleburne.com/podcast

Made in the USA
Lexington, KY
15 November 2019